P9-CAN-603

Simeon

POEMS BY

Donald Finkel

Atheneum
NEW YORK
1964

Some of these poems have appeared in ATLANTIC, the BRITISH POETRY SOCIETY ANNUAL (1962), CARLETON MISCELLANY, CHELSEA, EPOCH, HUDSON REVIEW, MASSACHUSETTS REVIEW, NOBLE SAVAGE, PARIS REVIEW, PERSPECTIVE, POETRY, POETRY NORTHWEST, QUARTERLY REVIEW OF LITERATURE, THIN LINE and TRANSATLANTIC REVIEW.

Library of Congress catalog card number 64–23296
Published simultaneously in Canada by
McClelland & Stewart Ltd.
Manufactured in the United States of America by
H. Wolff Book Manufacturing Co., Inc.
Designed by Harry Ford
First Edition

For Constance

Contents

FOUR

FIVE

One

Simeon *or* The Death of God

THE LAST (AND ONLY) LETTER FROM SIMEON'S HAND, ON HIS EJECTION FROM THE MONASTERY

It occurred to me today that God is subhuman.

Why does that shock you so? If we cannot
do what He thinks we ought, or acts as if,
then what is the earthly difference whether our failure
lies at the door behind us or the one before?

Locked in the cell of manhood, behold the man!
He yearns for childhood with every child he sees,
though his own had been unspeakable. And God
knows what he thinks when he sees a cat, or a bird.

I embrace him, the beast in me: he is my past.
My future also. Try not to worry.

S.

THE BROTHER'S APOLOGY

I had to have something to lift me from the garbage of my days.
The Arab has his hashish, the soldier his danger,
the codger his childhood, children their tears, the rich
their gold, visits, masquerades; the poor
have their hunger and children, merchants their losses,
and wives their vegetables and chatter. It all
drifts up to me where I sit, like burning garbage,
the cries, laughter, wagons, animals, ashes.

The old, as I said, have their childhood. Up from the gnarled
ailing feet, the ropy veins, the long
slack scrotum, the fallen belly, the breasts
like paper lanterns hung too long in the weather;
up from the bedpans and hernias, the hacking, hawking,
the rotten, or false, or no, teeth, the rheumy
eyes, from the yellowy hair, rises the faint
odorless dream of what they were; or what
they were not, who can be sure? They remember childhood
as a monk remembers women: something attainable,
had or not had, what matter? in another life,
by the man one could have been, if one had not
been saddled from the very beginning with being oneself.

So I remember Simeon, my brother.
I turn to his image as to a glimmer of childhood,
or a photograph of some naked untouchable woman.
As if, out of this scrabbling, screaming, screwing,
eating, sweating, I might drift up to him,
incinerated, white, weightless, nothing.
Is it strange such rotten flesh as his should seem
a haven from my own decay? His garbage
is not my garbage, his wound, remembered,
is clean as chiselled stone. His fetor rises
metaphysical as wind, his handkerchief
takes on the perfection of laundry: spit as he will,
it is no less perfect.

Can you wonder then why I need him?
why I hate him, as the codger hates the child?
as the cold priest hates the lover? I sit in the dark
stall of my flesh and wait for his confession.
He comes, he is the man: how can I forgive him?

EXPLANATORY

Once there were two brothers: Simeon,
and Simeon's brother. It may seem ironic to some
that Simeon's name should come down to us, while the brother's
is completely lost; since only the brother ever
learned how to write. But of the two, Simeon
was clearly the more resourceful. He saw quite early
the vanity of fame, and settled instead
for a comfortable notoriety.

Since the seed
of honor is pride, which germinates best in the dark,
he set about scratching like a crow to lay it bare.
After several years of this, during which, it is said,
his terrible practices caused his brethren to judge him
'unsuited to any form of community life,'
he deposited the result of his labors atop
a pillar, exposed to all men's speculation.

Thereon he performed, until the hour of his death,
continuously and free of charge, his various
functions as a man. Not much of an act;
yet it brought the crowds. He seemed, like the mountebank
and the dancing girl, to offer more and more.

The effect of this outdoor life was in general salubrious.
He managed to live his allotted three-score and ten;
although after a time his scent turned suspiciously high.
Something about him innately rotten, perhaps
(his wound, his mind), began to open like some
nocturnal flower, and poisoned the dreams of the city.

Meanwhile, the brother, who had never learned
to manage his life with Simeon's chaste perfection,
shuffled on, seven days a week, payday to payday,
as dignified as a beggar brandishing pencils.
It is from his hand we receive this little collection.

Or what remains. It is hard to believe he wrote
nothing after this. As if Simeon's death
and his own all but coincided. Or did he refuse
that gambit, and return, poor wandering Jew,
to his dry goods and his wife? Rimbaud of the Bronx,
Judas with a weekly paycheck, you can almost see him.

1: THE PILLAR

Stone. Kernel of solitude. Indifferent
to pain, pleasure, climate, place, emotion.
Stone. Concentration of forces, center of balance,
inward and outward the same, condition of rest.

Erect. Proud as a phallos. As innocent,
free of deception, of the gnarled indecent fig.
Erect. Human, male, arrogant, absolute,
raised like a mailed fist against the sky.

2: THE PROVENANCE OF THE STONE

Taller than he by half, heavier by ten,
surely he couldn't have managed it alone.
Friends? He had none, it was against his religion.
Samaritans? To judge from the legends, they stopped
for nothing less than a god, of course in disguise.
Mockers? Certainly not, mockers never carry
anything heavier than a feather, a needle, a pen.
Shrewd hardheaded men, these would have expected
some fair return, the Word, a cut of the profits.
Who were these strangers then, who was it bore
his stone like a gift to the place of his sacrifice?

Of course it is always possible he found it waiting;
for a saint all circumstances are propitious,
if only after the fact. But the question remains:
whose was it first? And what had they propped it under
to keep from falling on their heads, a temple? a tomb?
Surely in all the accounts there is one word
concerning the fate of these men, whose sweat and science
raised the tower he shinnied to consummation.

FIRST FOOTNOTE

The pillar was actually the middle finger
of the left hand of the Colossus of Rhodes.
With it Simeon contrived, before an assemblage
of 1000 Arabs, the Emperor Theodosius, and his mother,
in the firmest, most unambiguous manner possible,
to suggest to man what he could do with his life.

3: THE ANGEL

1

Some, soldiers of fortune, go forth to slay
the dimwitted monster Will with the pebble Whim.
Feeble, unprepossessing Simeon applies
jiu-jitsu, lifts him up; cut from his sources,
limp as a newborn child, he waits to be killed.

2

He fattens us in his house, against our will.
We ripen in his eaves while he watches, we dangle in his face
our radiant tempting cheeks. We shall let go.
We shall poison him with our sweetness: as we fall, so shall he.

3

Is it the angel he wrestles to a draw? Some pleasure
in giving, this one in taking. No blame. How else
keep justice alive in the world, balance and beauty,
the sea against the land, lover against lover,
pressing the halves till they fuse? How keep the world whole?

Though the gift be missent, or unwitting, is this to be scorned?
Does the virtuous giver distinguish the grateful from the proud?
The angel cares nothing for gratitude; he pays
Abel, screws Cain, screws Abel: it is all one.
Throw him the flank or the entrails; he devours, he devours.

Stay. Wrestle with him at the fording; breast to breast,
all night you shall sway in the moonlight, grunting and sighing
like lovers and dying men: there is nothing to lose.

4

Or is it himself he wrestles, his feet he tips
in the air? Rebel against nature: himself: he suffers;
enjoys the suffering of others. He is a god
wrestling with flesh, his brother. Reeling, high
in no man's country, the rules of the game are his.

4: MONOLOGUE: THE WIFE

He was never much of what you would call a husband;
an animal maybe, a cat. Or a child; when I think
of the mothering he took, and the holding my peace, how many
mornings he found me, when he came in, as silent
and unquestioning as a house. Sometimes he came
to me then, he had to kneel, and kissed me like a boy.
Then the kiss turned into a whisper (with the kids inside).

How they smirked when he left; you'd think I couldn't content
    him.
I gave him ten times what he asked; that is, when he asked,
which wasn't often. Mostly, he prowled about
picking up ashtrays and riffling books like a kid
who'd just found what he was made for, and nobody to try it on.
He brought out the mother in me. Something else, too.

One morning he sat up and smiled: All right, I'm a bastard.
I don't deserve you. God knows I never said it,
in so many words. He walked out buttoning his shirt,
not grandly, mind you, that wasn't his way; more
as if he were going out for a stroll or a beer.

I look in the mirror, sometimes, queer how things change;
his sweet seed sown, his body of a boy run through me
like a river: now, for this mushroom, for this fusty
pocketbook of a thing, can I call him to task?

SECOND FOOTNOTE

For those who wonder how Simeon came to be married:
the legends tell of at least three stylites called Simeon.

The first and most famous is said to have converted a dragon;
of the Younger, little is known, and all of it boring,
though he claimed in a letter to have already been sitting
on a pillar when he lost the first of his baby teeth.
The third is hid in a cloud, lit only by his death,
when his pillar unfortunately acted as a lightning-rod.
Were there not others, still, of whom nothing is heard?
Do the legends fail us here, or in any respect?

The value of originality is suspect,
and the rite, to retain its potency, bears repeating.
There have been men since Adam's first uprising
who would shin up a tree, or a gallows, or a flagpole, and flutter
for hours, days, years, in the crowd's cruel weather.

Guileless, damn him, always the innocent;
grease of the calf still glistens on his mouth.

But now the cloud shambles off, dropping the sun
behind him on the sky like a fiery pancake
(Simeon's halo: he wears it with a difference).
I feel his shadow on me, I feel my face
screw up against the light, a leering mask.

Co-signer of my own free will, whose fault
is it they come to me for the rest of the payments?
By whose default is his house now my house,
his children my stepchildren, his wife my wife?

In every kitchen quarrel or green offense
I see my rights in question (though in this
their silence and restraint are above reproach).
I flourish each hour and paycheck like a gift.

Five days a week I pay off Simeon's debts,
on the weekends sulk in the study and scratch my epic.
Outside the children yowl for their milk and love,
and the wolf at the door (hear him?): *You owe! You owe!*

6: SIMEON AMONG THE RAINDROPS

It rained down on him, it gathered in his beard
and his eyebrows, and at the end of his nose. It clung,
fell away from him, clung. It got under his clout,
it trickled around his tool like a woman's finger.

He looked between the drops and saw the stones
raise imperceptibly their ancient backs to take
each drop as it came, in the fleeting second before
it ran down into the ground and lost itself.

He peered from the caves of his ears and heard it whisper;
from time to time he opened up his mouth
to let it in. It merged with the flow of his thoughts,
it crept to his center, it spread. He began to tremble
a little, then uncontrollably. He lost
himself in a bone-wrenching ecstasy. At last he was warm.

He knew the sickness, he gave in to its caress.
Like a boy's first case of clap, it would not kill him:
it was only an initiation, not an end.

7: SONG OF THE CONVERTED ISHMAELITES

WHAT DO YOU MEAN HE HAD A HARD TIME, HONEY. I HAD A HARD TIME. YOU HAD A HARD TIME. WE ALL HAD A HARD TIME.

THE LADY DOWNSTAIRS

Like the madman, he is sacred; he can insult the king.
He is a living reproach: beware of his wrath.
Shall we tell him to laugh away the smell of his wound?
Shall we tell him his shadow is a passing whim of the sun?
He will not be cajoled, or put off, nor his logic refuted.

Though he understands nothing, yet he provides understanding;
though he stinks like the ditch of hell, he is divine.
Staring into the depths of his wound we worship
all that is mortal, passive, empty of meaning;
we cannot ignore his suffering, it is our own.

Yet were he instead to claim joy, we would slay him forthwith;
for who but a fool could believe him? Who, even granting,
could abide for long the chatter of a shining face?

Standing in his long shadow we are as children;
for we are made in his image: dumbfounded we listen.
In the silence, it is always possible we shall hear
the sound of our own hearts' beating, some news of ourselves.

8: THE PILLARS CONTINUE TO INCREASE IN HEIGHT

The first was all of a piece, a nine-foot finger
blown from the mother cliff. He made it up
in a leap and a scrabble; the air was fresh, the shadows
sharper, blacker, things drew in their edges.

At the point of focus he paused. But there is no pausing;
each day calls forth reaffirmation: he climbs.
The air grows thin, he weakens. As well, he sighs,
be giddy now as later in dotage: upward!

9: SIMEON NEARS HIS TIME

Already the fluids settle, on his feet
great blisters form and ooze, his final illness;
at the last, a dry leaf on a barren tree,
he will release his hold, and be blown away.

A Job who went out looking for his boils:
will God stand by for this? will there be this time
an explanation, or double your money back?

To these questions the skies are silent as usual.
Actually, Simeon has asked for nothing, he has taken the boils
before, or as, they were given. He moves with the punch;
he turns the other cheek, and moves again.
If this is punishment, he takes it like a reward.

Yet walk out in the street: the crowd threatens,
it raises against you its soiled pragmatic fist.
Up there, the blow is real, the boot in the can;
the moment of contact, however, is drawn out for years.
In such tranquillity, terror is recollected,
rejection made bearable, taken a grain at a time.

IF YOU DON'T SEE WHAT YOU WANT, ASK FOR IT.

The time of forthrightness is past, the out-
and-out miracle: Damn it, I need some light;
and there was light. The honest rod pulsing
with miracles, the pubes in sunlight, moist
and miraculous as a garden. No longer the stolen
fruit tastes sweet, no longer the honest
stone is raised in the quarrel, nor raised
the arm of the honest lie at the stones of the crowd.
The priest turns judge, the repentant thief goes free;
the hero rides for pay. At the foot of the stone
the crowd leaps in his horny hand like a spear.

I knew a fellow once who used to eat
his apple, flesh, stem, seeds, all;
inexorable and fastidious as a god, nothing
escaped him, not the least trickle of sweetness,
not the last bitter miracle in her pod.
A true philosopher, an honest man, where has he gone?

These days it's with me or against, either hate
or love, shit or get off the pot. A committee
came yesterday with papers, demanding: the stink
of his ferment assails the public air, the safety
of children is threatened; they would pluck him down
and toss him in the bin. To be honest, I don't
know what I think. Some nights, in this heat,
lying with my face to the window for the faint night
breeze, I catch a whiff of him, and the old rage
rises in my chest. I think, What is that bastard
doing to me? But it passes. Everything passes;
little by little the night breeze carries it away.

11: THE WOUND

A priest once came who doubted Simeon's substance.
Simeon's head jerked once: a beckoning?

The priest labored up. On hands and knees for the height,
he gazed on a wound as large as a woman's mouth,
red, depthless, open.

Far below,
each man and stone became itself, distinct,
literal, plain, like the breasts of a woman in moonlight.

THIRD FOOTNOTE

A legend persists among the Arabs Simeon had hidden
under his clout an image of the goddess of Minos,
which he brought out only when he thought he was alone.
By the time he had reached sixty feet no one could tell
where Simeon left off and the heathen idol began.
Or what he was doing. When they reached him, he had left
but one great wound, from which his life had poured.
The goddess of Minos was nowhere to be seen.

12: DIALOGUE CONCERNING THE WIFE

SIMEON:
The priestess of Minos arranges her limbs to ease
the passage of my delight, and we are gone
bobbing along the blood to the drowning sea.
From night to night we drift with the tides like the dead.

BROTHER:
A certain human clumsiness and certain
purely personal blemishes contrive
to slow and stir my beating blood at once.
There is no perfection possible. But there is tomorrow.

13: SIMEON'S SONG

Praised be the six holes of sense, where the mind's fingers grope;
praised be the hollow of balance, where beauty hides;
praised be the gully of need, whose fleshy flowers,
eaten, but remind the appetite of what it seeks.

Praised be the shaft of my sex, I follow it to the end.
Praised be the anus, doorway of revelation;
behind you the rites of change are conducted in darkness,
in your steamy rift the smith beats his ore into life.
And praised be the mouth, omnivorous as God,
of flanks, entrails, smoke, sleeping-pills, anti-freeze;
tunnel of delight, ditch of our sustenance: hide me.

14: THE SUN

It burned him to a char of wick, to the irreducible,
the no longer vulnerable, that which no longer can be
imposed upon, or changed. Also, he was dead.

He may still have thought; there was no way of knowing. When
had his senses so made one with the ardent weather,
they might as well have been the weather? So,

it was hard to decide when to bury him; if at all.
For the sun had already accomplished whatever the dark
lady of worms could do in her house. Better.

He smelled not at all, resembled nothing, either
to pity or loathe, he offended no one. Really,
it was hard enough to remember he was once a man.

15: THE DEATH OF SIMEON

He knew the sea that lapped at the shore of his ear.
All things impinged alike, pleasures and pains,
his own or someone else's, a woman's, a people's.
He acknowledged the insults and did not disavow
the praise, or the exaggerations, either.

He suffered them to come. He heard the whisper
of the drowned, mermaids and sailors; all things took on
the phosphorescence of dreams and dying fish.

Lady of Minos, he cried, sea of grape, bowl of honey,
breast whereon Odysseus foundered, source
of my first cry, sphinx of my difficulty, mother:
long have I drifted, come, let me probe your dark
with my winnowing oar. Again I shall father forth
children, furniture, debts, populations, war.

In the distance he heard the crowd roar like a triton:
Father, Simeon, why dost thou forsake us?
He smiled, lay back as if spent, and let go of his soul.

Or have I the right to think, in the end, he doubted?
At the brink where man turns god, what darkness falls?
It is not revenge: that ignorance was his
humanity. It was the god I hated.

Two

A WALK IN THE COUNTRY

FOR R.B.

After two weeks I was sick with emotion,
a rash on my neck, here, and under my eyes;
in the morning the maid came and found me,
one look, and she screamed: *Indigestione!*
In a city so beautiful, beautiful! to be ugly,
red, a disease! I bought nothing but—scarves.
She runs her long tense fingers back from her throat
on both sides, letting them stay where they meet.

Beyond, a mole rustles under the leaves,
stiffens, wrinkling his fastidious nose;
a bluejay leaps like a clown on a fallen birch,
then crashes away, rattling the shadows.
To be ugly, he thinks, in that soft gray light,
where with her confident fingers beauty gestures
in the galleries, the shops, the market, row on row,
red, orange, yellow, miraculous fruit!

But beauty is not beauty that remains
unaltered in the face of further beauty;
brightness and darkness, marriage of sky and earth,
make of the soft gray light in the human city
something the flickering bluejay understands,
something the mole acknowledges, then slips,
at the first, faint tremble of her approach,
shyly, like a heart into silence, underground.

THE STRANGER: 1

Time and again he would return to that sleep,
but she draws him back with her body, with her whiteness,
with the confident health of her gestures as she dances.
Naked from the waist she dances, in the afternoon darkness,
in the round flickering room of the afternoon.

His arms about his knees, almost unborn,
he watches out of the darkness her flashing breasts;
then, like a sob, he rises, his arms before him;
he moves from shadow to shadow, toward the world's dancing.

THE STRANGER: 2

The woman is a darkness on which light plays.
Like the moon, like a swimmer at night, she moves through
an element of which she knows herself to be part.
Sweet wisdom; to his watching eyes the light
that darts along her limbs seems self-contained.

Having lost, until death, the natural knowledge of darkness
adrift among flittering lights, without intending,
the stranger announces himself with a creaking oar.
The bodies flash and fade. Rocking, he sits;
behind his back in the trees the darkness giggles.

I am neither as innocent nor as untrusting as an animal;
the irascible bear, and the chipmunk, scrambling
a dozen times back before stealing my crusts,
have managed to penetrate this deeper than I have.

I know all poisons by name, I can draw meat
safely out of the most delicate snare;
my brain is an attic of unusable antidotes.
I am prepared, in short, for anything but wisdom.

You, who confuse ignorance with concentration,
who worship distance and length, who cry out nightly
to the great blond creator of mountains and frescoes,
you will fail, I know, to appreciate my condition.

You are not insensible, it's true, insolence touches you;
murder, lust, sloth, in sufficient degree,
sets one taut string whining like a mosquito.
I dream of setting fire to your museums.

The bluejay screams, twice, and then twice again;
a storm is brewing, chipmunk and bear return
to their separate darkness, my crusts lie in the door.

And now the first whispers, electric distractions;
laughing in the mountains through his red beard,
your insolent giant begins to rattle his lumber.

LETTER FOUND IN A THERMOS BOTTLE

MA VIE NE FUT QUE FOLIES DOUCES, C'EST REGRETTABLE

Some days I can't help peeking at the papers,
like one who cannot wait for his water to boil;
ogres are grappling in the distant mountains,
they howl threats, one has uprooted an oak
and is brandishing it. A hush falls on the plain:
o sweet enfolding silence! o last month's papers!

Prayer I have tried, cold showers, ten-day diets,
Zen, psychiatry, mushrooms, marriage, chess.
One time I practiced abstinence, total: ate not,
drank not, slept not, walked not; after a month
the beating of my heart, the wheeze of my lungs
had grown so loud in my ears I had to stop.

And crime? don't speak of it; I have tried
a little of everything, stealing, pimping, murder,
even the major atrocities, art, self-pollution.
The police have given me up; the sums, negligible,
have found their way back into circulation;
the bodies, on the other hand, have never been found.

Even work, even virtue itself, would perhaps be bearable,
if only one could give himself to it, wholly,
with all the submission and delicacy of a geisha.
Yet, once in a while, a demand comes, so unspeakable
that, afterward, I relish, sprawling among the stains,
a few hours the prisoner's childlike sleep.

FOR NOAH, MY SON, SLEEPING

Ferrying souls across from a drowning world,
and cattle, horses, they came, each hearing in his ear
his personal omen, to the new found land,
the country discovered by blunder, like beauty, and death.

And truly, there was in the mines more gold than earth;
angels like savage children brought them death, and gifts.
Exhausting the mines, soon they tired of the gold;
facing the death, they escaped the resurrection.

Yet it is men like those on whom the dying depend
to carry them safe, over the womanly sea,
until they sight to leeward, springing like fact,
the country they have been sailing backward to reach.

Sitting on this dusty bench, here by the inn,
I play a kind of dreaming Rip to your Hendrick;
I think of you playing games with your little friends,
and wait here, telling stories, till you come out.

Noah in your moonboat, Hendrick in your halfmoon,
sleeping under the mountain till the sea rise again.

COCTEAU'S *OPIUM*: 1

EVEN WITHOUT ANY SPIRIT OF PROSELYTIZING, IT IS IMPOSSIBLE FOR A PERSON WHO DOES NOT SMOKE TO LIVE WITH A PERSON WHO DOES. EACH WOULD INHABIT A DIFFERENT WORLD.

Still, no one has paid much tribute to the man
who has to live *in* the addict, that madman, that poet,
that adolescent pimpled with spiritual acne;
to support him, and his wife, and his brats,
to purchase with sweat his fixes and his furniture.
Lorenzo de' Medici. Solomon Guggenheim. Pah!

And for what? But it is like trying to turn your back
on a sick cat. There is a kind of man
who cannot keep from carrying one home.

The addict, on the other hand, needs no excuse;
does he say, The world is chaos, therefore I need
my opium, my art, my ivory, my politics, my morals?
At the crucial moment, he says nothing.
He knows the world *is* order, because he knows
each scrap of chaos personally, by first name.

It is the Judas in Jesus, reason, the eternal husband,
who at the end, having paid the rent for so long,
begins to wonder if it is possible he has been forsaken.

THE LEITMOTIV OF DE PROFUNDIS. THE ONLY CRIME IS TO BE SUPERFICIAL. EVERYTHING WHICH IS UNDERSTOOD IS GOOD. THE REPETITION OF THIS SENTENCE IS IRRITATING AND REVEALING.

Picasso, who knows everything, will tell you:
everything is a miracle; for instance, that one
does not dissolve in one's bath "like a lump of sugar."
Everywhere, euphoria of opium, euphoria of art,
everywhere the equation of miracle with understanding,
true with beautiful, wise with good.

The miracle blasts the fig tree, from which it expects
the impossible; it demands to be understood; it has all
the significance of a man kicking a cat. It is the blind
damning the blind for not being able to conduct
a guided tour in this country of miracles. *De profundis,*
in the place of suffering, where everything is understood.

Like the noble fig, let us accept our punishment;
"a tree must suffer from the rising of its sap."
Certainly we have not been good; innocence, like ignorance,
is no excuse. Ask the adolescent, ask the addict
taking the cure, or the first weed of spring;
every morning, rising, rising, rising, ask yourself.

"MY PAINTING WILL NEVER OFFEND"

RAPHAEL

The way Beatrice does not offend, perhaps,
she chides you for your own good; the way
Circe does not offend, it is the smell
of the other pigs that assails your nostrils.

However there is always the danger of replacing
the beau ideal with the least common denominator,
the true Rheingold Girl, so inoffensive as
to be completely invisible, odorless, a Virgin.

No martyrdoms, no Last Judgments, and after one or two
youthful indiscretions, no crucifixions either;
he who had seen the streets splash in the blood
of Grifone's victims, and then in Grifone's,
preoccupied with the harmony of gestures.

Not to offend Jesus is one thing; not to offend Judas,
another. Judas has paid for his good manners
with a sensitive stomach. Everything offends him.
Something simple please, chopped steak and a baked potato.
Jesus, on the other hand, has a stomach like a boiler;
where he hangs, nothing can offend him but himself.

Yet if we could smell her out, that Lady of Silences,
who can lead men, at her whim, to heaven or hell,
resigned to be saints or satisfied to be swine;
she would bring a peace like the Son of God,
not in his aspect of Florence Nightingale, nor either
wearing Marx's whiskers over his goatee,
but as that god of women, Dionysus,
wearing nothing but an archaic smile,
and, over his article, a cluster of purple nipples.

THE SERPENT CHARMER

(AFTER JEAN LEON GÉRÔME)

This smooth stripling wears nothing but a snake,
festoons of the beast ripple along his back
and thighs; the head he holds aloft, it is
too somnolent to raise itself alone.
Gérôme has shown us all this elsewhere:
the Turkisch lady who crouches at the bath;
over her head the black and harsh-clothed maid
begins to tip an urn of freezing water;
and in the market-place a buyer rubs
his hard forefinger on the slave-girl's teeth.

A violent story, beauty and the beast;
yet what a curious dryness in the telling.
Or is it meticulous love, that dotes as long
on the lovely inscrutable arabic on the wall
as on the sheikh who sprawls against it, among
his half-wild men. Yet finally, here is the source
of dryness, of beauty and beast, of love, of hate:
watching the naked boy and snake, this face
under the black tarboosh is a snarl of delight.

CALL OF THE CALL-GIRLS

FOR N.M.

Has anyone here seen Odysseus, that cocksure sailor,
curly-headed Odysseus, back from the war,
whom any witch would give her secret for?
In what dark harbor has he been perfecting
his technique, squat daddy, wandering phallos?
Go tell him, it is our pasture he has been seeking;
he passed here once, next time he will know better.

About men we know something; these bones could tell you,
these white bones by us bleaching in the sun,
these sweet, sea-faring, roistering, drunken bones.
Let them tell you about this man, who can't sit still,
this great white serpent, swimming from harbor to harbor:
he thinks, being all man, that he will escape us,
a free spirit floating upon our waters,
he thinks he can come, and go. He is mistaken.

Subject to every tweak of time, and prey
to war, disease, low blows, sunburn, old age,
tell him, warn him; no matter, he cannot hear,
for every day he sails closer to perfection.
Louder and louder our song grows in his ears;
this one, so goes the refrain, is the be-all and end-all.
Never again will he have to go back to his wife;
he will stand there forever, tied to his own mast,
throbbing away, without a thought in the world.

The angel is, perhaps, a sore loser,
seeing no humor in the outcome of the match.
Still, one wonders, why on earth pick on Jacob?
A weak link in the chain, yes (but not
quite weak enough, in a way, for his own good).

As always, petty thief to the end, Jacob
can't shake off fully his fondness for things, can never
blot out his mother's promptings.
Aboriginal
Jerome, out for a stroll in the desert, he meets
the angel, pauses a moment to chat. Suddenly
he is seized with alarm; all night they wrestle there,
until morning lights up his face like common sense.
He walks to the nearest city, and his wife.

THE EFFECT OF THE POEM

The effect of the poem, like opium, is immediate.
The good patient downs his placebo and waits
for something; preferably negative, a cheap thrill.

But the poem, like salvation, does not come cheap.
Immediate, yes, and nothing down; the payments, however,
continue the rest of your life. For this reason

most people, like tragic heroes, would rather wait
until the last possible minute before purchasing any.

This the addict knows, and the saint, and the true
religious martyr (whom we must not confuse
with the masochist who blunders into a church),

and this the learned astronomer knows, who walks
into a manhole while tallying his stars.

THE FLAGPOLE SITTER

1

Slowly the world contracts about my ears.
First morality goes, then love, then fear
of my death; then beauty, which is bearable truth,
then truth unbearable; then pleasure, then pain.
Rocking at last in the irreducible sun,
slowly, more slow, more slow, I leave behind
even the memory that I was ever a man.

2

Like a shadow passing over the brain, from back to front,
a cool silver, a heat that looks like coolness as it runs,
molten, over the dipping ladle; this is not sleep,
but a gliding darkness, a shadow conscious of nothing
but itself, yet knowing that so intensely, it is bright.

3

When the wind blows,
a few leaves fall to the ground;
where have I been?

4

From those fat green burghers, nodding their hundred chins
at the wind's words, conspiratorial whispers,
I purchased nothing; I passed among their wares
taking nothing, wanting nothing, looking for the exit.
How did I find that city of mossy gutters?
Keeping always to my room, I was poorly prepared,
soothed by the safety of angles, the wisdom of corners
where three unruffled surfaces agree.
One moment of absence, and down the alley,
before me and behind, that army of
obscene salesmen, vegetable, complacent,
plucking at my shirt with their green fingers.

5
Seeing it, I am no longer part of it.
Part of it no longer, I forfeit the right
to be a paradigm. Forfeiting that right,
I become totally free.

6
I have begun to know the true weight of my body.
Slowly the fluid settles in my legs;
it seeps into my shoes, great blisters form,
my final illness. My rivers run into the air;
at the last, a dry leaf on a barren tree,
I shall release my hold, and be blown away.

In the American dream it is customarily deleted
along with odors, tooth decay, and the clap,
in a shy bid for the approval of Parents' Magazine.

The Greeks could not find a place for it
on their marble, though the Babylonians
managed to tattoo it on their humbler clay.

It is something woman would much rather forget,
this net, this trap, this tangled labyrinth
where lurks the outcome of her beastliness.

Or is this veil the riddle of the princess,
the answer to which is the lovely princess herself?
Behind the darkness at the door, the door is dark.

There is another version of the story,
in which the answer to the riddle is the man.
"Who comes?" she asks, half animal, half human.

"I come," he replies, "whenever I get the chance.
It is I, crawling, walking, limping, here I come;
the third leg is not necessarily a walking stick."

For there is no difference between the Sphinx and Jocasta,
riddle and prize; one kills all who do not
know the answer, the other all who do.

Still, the fellow comes, eager to penetrate
any mystery, whether of death or birth.
If you ask him, in fact, he will explain

that it was he in the first place who designed
the labyrinth, as a kind of school
for heroes, artificers, and mice.

NOTE IN LIEU OF A SUICIDE

IN THOSE DAYS THEY SHALL SAY NO MORE, THE FATHERS HAVE EATEN A SOUR GRAPE, AND THE CHILDREN'S TEETH ARE SET ON EDGE.

I am surrounded by armies, I have sent them word
it was not I who asked for a fight.
By whose decree am I called Jew?
By my grandfather's who observed the passover?
They have sent word back it was not they.
By my father's who knows a few yiddish jokes?
I shake my fist at the sky and there is no lightning.
By the local rabbi's who has recognized my name?
I have just looked in the ark and found a stone.

Yet since when have I not been a Jew?
Since the day I heard God was dead?
The blood is on me, I am not clean.
Since the day I became a Unitarian?
Like a woman in her time I am not clean.
Since the day I first discovered that in these
perilous times every man jack is circumcised?
Like a dog that has rolled in dogshit I am not clean.
The blood on my hands is as much his
as the blood in my veins. Admitted.

I will leave the silver in the temple,
but I am damned if I will hang myself;
I have in Kerioth a wife and two kids
who but for me would be living on the state.

of the lonely sniper from the land with a language all questions,
to whom it is natural, peering at the curved blade of the moon,
to say (to himself, of course, rubbing with his beardless jaw
the stock of his weapon), "Moon?" To whom it is not
in the least strange, feeling at his cheek the oiled coolness
of walnut in the night (in a whisper as thin as the moon's kris),
to say, "Wood?" To say, "Weapon?" To say (or really not to say,
to find said, a thought as faint as the old moon dying
on the edge of the new), "Death?" And to watch as, hesitantly,
then surer and surer, bright bullets in the black answer,
"Yes. Yes. Yes."

Three

THE HYPOCHONDRIAC

Stretched out like a drunk in the dark he listens
to the wash of his insides and tries to catch the rhythm,
hoping by cautious breathing and the right thought
at the appropriate moment to keep from submitting,
not, not, at any cost, to be sick.

Now the tide sucks downward to his groin,
beginning a duller though more controllable pain;
but it is only momentary, it will be back
lapping in frothy wavelets at his throat.

He would go to the mountains, but it is so far,
and the climbing, the strenuous games in the thin air
would distract him, shatter his concentration,
spewing among the startled sunburnt guests
all he has been saving hidden for years.

The commerce between mind and flesh is a trickle at best,
and who knows better than he what chaos awaits
the body gone unminded even a second.

LOSS OF HEARING

His news lies only at the crests
of what we tell: he bobs in shallows
mostly, and considers. Hears
of islands from the chariest birds;
what castles does he raise from their
least droppings? Craft that cross him where
he drifts come always purposely:
the gam's an awkward business. Lines
fall short, wind takes your words
and wrings them. Equally to cries,
to silence, a bland smile across
the heaving distance: scant reward
for voyage half so perilous.

Of what we choose to float at him
he makes a jetsam world we could
never have thought ourselves. The winds
conspire to cheat him. But who says
from off what continent our cries
are lofted? In the highlands we
from peak to peak return in kind

echo for echo faithfully.
Who says out there the wind is more
capricious than what whips us here?

MYOPIC

If you come close enough to him
the corners of his mouth will twitch
as if by strings, since like a match
before him your familiar face
has flared a moment earlier.

He treads a road he hardly sees,
you would not tread for fear to fall
through perilous interstices.
Under his stare the roadside stone
unbends its stubborn boundaries
as not to bruise him, and the trees
draw their vindictive fingers in.
He knows he cannot come to harm,
for, like the infant, what he sees
is part of him; until he puts
his bottle lenses on and lets
the world spring up and scratch at him.

Meanwhile, like summer clouds we blunder
along the verges of his view,
and take the shapes he thinks we do;
and all he hears when we collide
is reassuring distant thunder.

TWO STEPS OF A LAME MAN

His leg is arched about a sphere
of air which leaps evenly between
his gallopings. He moves like a worn
centaur in the grove behind a temple.
The bright sphere lifts against his loins
and he soars. But he is too much child
of the ground and, pah! he returns
in a harsh arc, a centaur rampant
too long, by the gates of the temple.

The sphere is a virgin of air
against his loins, and the keen
of her kiss sends him rearing. Torn
between head and hooves, between temple
and the sweat of seed, he careens
on his wry limb in a wild
reel, grace of the muskiest wines.
Bereft of virgin then, and cursed by balance,
crashes among the trees that hide the temple.

THE FAIRY IN THE NEXT CHAIR

The fairy in the next chair is telling
his barber about Horace. (He was a
better poet, only he was so *cold.*)

Whereas the man on my hair told
me that winter was here. Outside
a cold rain is preparing to fall.

With difficulty, and probably in
some peril of shipwreck, Horace
returned to Rome. At Philippi, his

shield lay where he threw it. Praise
to Mercury, who in a mist huddled
him to safety. Outside the mist is

hardening into rain. The barber has
confided to me that he likes a drink
now and then (for the cold) but it is

bad for business. Business is bad
all over. In the next chair the
fairy is telling the man about

restraint. Outside the winter edges
the day with rain. Business is bad
all over (excess and restraint). Squat

Horatius cautions against avarice. Behold,
what infamy and ruin rise from a large
dish. Cold Flaccus remembers his shield

in Macedon, remembers the instruction of
hunger. Now my rhyming heat is cooled.
Outside the rain practices a cold restraint.

WISH YOU WERE HERE

In a village that hangs shimmering in heat
against the hills (as against a monastery
wall a hanging of the holy city
shivers to the wind of passing sisters)
two black crones against the plaster
world reap corn from stone and gather
black beans in the factitious street.

In a village like a postcard one tall street
climbs from the market to the cemetery,
stone by stone a shrewd asymmetry.
Someone has been too careful here, some master
has painted over-long: the reds are over-
red, the clouds are cotton and will never
let fall invention through the teemless heat.

This is the village we dreamed of in the heat
of somebody else's summer, this is the city
from which the postcard came: a view of twenty
churches, orange, mango, jacaranda.
Now in a village of unending summer
a small wind stirs where twenty withered fingers
scuttle like hungry spiders in the street.

TO PROFESSOR SO-AND-SO

After three hundred years had I not grown
content with my oblivion and found
solace in small needs satisfied—one song,
one line, that ran like Rhenish from the jar,
or one wool-merchant's wife who otherwise
had gone into her grave and never learned
the long sweet shudder of a metaphor—
when, groping among old coats in a dusty closet,
you closed your hand upon another hand?

Plagued by the image of some upcountry virgin
lending in furnished rooms translucent limbs
to how many fumbling hands, and all for love;

suffering, like some old codger halfway woman,
himself the insolence of every youth
who lingers in a doorway, or jeers from a crowd;

he drank his life into a towering rage,
reeled from woman to woman, marrying some,
and wrote, to feed his face, erotic books.

ORACLE

It is I, Orpheus, speaking through a mouthful of dust;
to hell with Apollo, I can keep still no longer.
Listen, Finkel, stop piecing me together
in your bounding iambics. Besides, you read too much;

the tune the stones will dance to is not in the books.
Inside your wife is sleeping, with fine long legs,
whom Hades has not yet noticed. While there is time,
get off your ass and make the most of her.

The Hero

THE GARDEN

THE HERO'S MOTHER IS A ROYAL VIRGIN; HIS FATHER IS A KING.

Tuesday and Friday evenings at half-past five
regular as an alarm the doorbell rammed
my heart against my shoulder-blades. I opened,
suffered the scrape of that determined kiss;
and kissed him back. That was my end of it. Still,
lugging his coat into my mother's room,
I think I sensed his part was only the harsh
reflection of my own: to play at once
the stranger and the king in his own house.
Softly I laid that coat on my mother's bed
and turned and marched into the living room.

Sundays we drove, in good weather, out in the country,
alone among traffic, unspeaking, like fugitives,
grimly took notice of trees, sniffed at the dogwood;
spring jammed us together in a garden of shifts and clutches.
Squeezed in the vise of that silence it seemed to me
they had shared in the past, not simple knowledge, but flesh.
Like twins joined at the breast they had drunk of each other;
now must they turn to speech, merely because
someone (so they might live) had wrenched them apart?

Once, coming back, I opened the door for a flower;
a cider-jug crashed in the roadway. Wordless with choler,
for a moment he choked on something; then he hit me.
We sat there silent in the odor of ripening apples.

EXILE IN EGYPT

AN ATTEMPT IS MADE TO KILL HIM, BUT HE IS SPIRITED AWAY, AND REARED BY FOSTER PARENTS IN A FAR COUNTRY.

Dreams stood me in good stead, there in that country.
In the land of my affliction, nobody murmured,
'Behold, this dreamer cometh.' Safe for a time
from the pit, the knife to throat, the stealing, selling,
in a household of women slowly I perfected my weapons:
weaving, saving, tenderness, small deceit;
but weakness in special, my one true advantage.

Weakness in all forms I made work for me.
(Though not, like women, simply by brandishing;
rather, giving when pressed, conceding, admitting,
winning, shameless, by small retreats. But winning.)
Let the strong man waggle his fist, I back off rhyming;
let the wise man floor me with fact, him I confound
with the quick disarming grin of a metaphor.

Far from my father's business, a while I kept
the seven lean years at bay. And even there,
in the time of hunger, it was dreams that saved me.

WE ARE TOLD NOTHING OF HIS CHILDHOOD.

We are told every trifle, soon or late;
what we hear is quite another matter.
The cries of Phalaris' victims, whom he roasted
over a slow fire in a brazen bull,
fell like soft music on the tyrant's ear.

And what of the shrieking children in the street,
pressing the sheriff's quest, the outlaw's trial?
The game is music but the cries are real.

THE RETURN

ON REACHING MANHOOD HE RETURNS TO HIS FUTURE KINGDOM.

I stop at the edge of the field and he comes out running,
his face blown out; his dignity flies to the wind.
He throws his arms around me. I stand here
smelling his bad teeth, bearing no rancor.
His hands pat, pat on my back, for no words come:
I hold my little speech and wait for the moment.

He is shouting. I know that voice. When I was small
he sent me inside with it once to wash my hands.
Weeping, my hands unreal under the water,
I cried to the Lord to drown him in that basin.
When I came out he was standing by the door:
'You are not my son,' he said. 'A son would love me.
I am not wanted here.' He opened the door
and left. I know that voice. He is shouting;
already at all the windows faces appear,
the door opens, my arrival is a fact.

The women are all questions. I have a mind, almost,
to tell them where I have been, the tall trucks booming
down the night, the nights under porches, the nights
outside roadhouses, the nights inside. I have
a mind almost to tell them, but it is all right,
they will not wait for an answer: too much has happened
in the meantime to them. And suddenly in the doorway
that one last face; I raise my eyes to those
indignant eyes. The old man goes, placating,
in a voice I have not heard, but now I know it.

And how should I tell those eyes it is a mistake,
that never pleaded for a thing, or wept into water?
That I plunged my hands into a quivering face,
and the face dissolved? Can I say I have not come back?

In the kitchen the fire flares up at the dripping calf;
I have come back. Is it worth it to tell those eyes
how the house is a different house, how that cracked voice
changes each minute from the voice I knew?

I said it there in the field, but no one listened:
I was wrong in the eyes of heaven, and in his eyes,
and though I have come back home, this is not home,
and that is not my father, nor this his son.

HE MARRIES A PRINCESS AND BECOMES A KING. FOR A TIME HE REIGNS UNEVENTFULLY.

The horses stand up again and shake themselves,
the flies stir on the wall, the fire brightens,
the maid goes on plucking the chicken, and the cook
gives such a slap to the scullery boy he yells.

For three years now it has been like that every morning;
and watching the horses wheel, the dogs in snow,
the thrill is not diminished. The wise were wrong:
you can never have too much of a good thing.

No, with a little luck, and moderate taxes,
it should keep going. Even in off years
the wine is passable; and who can kick
if the crops are plentiful and the people happy?

For a while I walked the corridors when I came.
In every room they hung like tapestries,
as if time had snagged on the nail of four o'clock,
at day's dead center, banal afternoon:

the throne-room empty but for one maid,
dusting and dusting a mantel; upstairs a guest
climbed forever into his dinner clothes;
neither the night begun nor the day ended.

And yet the dailiest gesture seemed to me,
simply by virtue of its hanging there,
translucent and inevitable and fine.
Even the dust stayed dancing in the sun

in formal patterns. I thought, And who am I
to blow like a wind behind such attitudes?
Having no use for perfection, however, they thank me.
Later in the tower, watching those little breasts

lift toward me imperceptibly, and fall,
I felt desire sprout in the dark like a tuber.
But bending my mouth to that perfect mouth I wondered
from what it was I had meant to save this kingdom.

BUT LATER HE LOSES FAVOR WITH THE GODS, AND MEETS WITH A MYSTERIOUS DEATH AT THE TOP OF A HILL.

That was a long row to hoe to reach this dung-heap,
Pangaion, Pisgah, Calvary, Parnassus;
but a wrench of the head, or the heart, one stick in the ribs,
and the bone turns music, and the flesh word.

I had a mild flame, I thought, though once in a while
it might have been, when I was singing, your voice
bouncing off the walls, your lightning at my fingers;
between those moments was a long hard time.

Down to the last wheeze and rattle, so it goes,
you come right to it, and I yell, I bleed;
here on the brink of Zion you forsake me.
Just once more, send me a sign, while I have eyes.

APOTHEOSIS

HIS CHILDREN, IF ANY, DO NOT SUCCEED HIM. HIS BODY IS NOT BURIED, BUT NEVERTHELESS HE HAS ONE OR MORE HOLY SEPULCHRES.

Toward the last he began to mistrust his friends.
The sound of his own voice soothed him, he wandered about
the country giving readings. Everywhere
he scattered into the miracle-famished crowd
bright loaves and fishes, for a moderate fee.
In the morning, however, one woke with a bitter taste,
and a dozen, perhaps, of hard inedible lines.

Now in a thousand attics red-eyed boys
wrestle his dicta. All night they travel his footsteps,
in the same taverns drink the identical drink;
homeward at morning, down the same dim street,
reeling a slope of nausea into bed.
Along the wall his fables sit like stones;
he rose (one hears) to heaven from one of these.

LETTER TO AN ALTO MAN

"Any note I want to, any time."
That's what you said, I think of it often.
Knees bent, hunched over your horn,
running your fingers up and down as if
over a row of hard golden nipples.

Nothing you do is wrong: it cries with pleasure!
(Between sets we lit up in the alley,
and walked about in the night where nobody fluffs.)

You were married, the last time I heard,
had a daughter, and drove to a thousand horns
a bus in South Chicago. I have a daughter.
(The same night fingers the bumps of Chicago,
though you or I stay home.) We do what we will.

Or might as well. Nothing we do is wrong:
solid, the notes rise in the smoky air,
one after the other, of their own accord.

After three years of the marriage-bed, what makes me
remember Mona on our block when I
was twelve, who had the mind of a four-year-old
and a body flexing to woman like a sergeant's arm,
and who on a certain Saturday afternoon
stepped down the aisle of a movie theater
over the bodies of several fallen boys,
allowing one terrible moment of muscular thighs
and a white-cotton-covered secret?

But
what I remember was Mona another day,
one white knee to the pavement, tying her shoe
in front of the appetizer store. O for just
one peep at that laundered secret I watched her
pull out the bow, and tie it, and pull it out;
then she peered slyly through her lank brown hair,
and satisfied I saw with what intricate ease
she managed those matters, she tied it once again.

SONG FOR SYRINX AND PENNYWHISTLE

He has a name halfway between
a bell and a snicker. Has a nose,
which often when he shaves he sees,
that, as a mountain rides the world,
rides on his face, self-conscious, sure,
a challenge to heroes. He is proud
of his blue eyes: he thinks they are green.

And the mouth, see: grins if you greet
him, hangs like that for half a street
onward, after you have gone.
It is well past smile, but half
refuses laugh, as if it might
loose on a world but half prepared
a furtive regiment of teeth.

It wrings his face until you see
past soaring corners to a pair
of pointed goat-fur-tufted ears.
But no, not so. This social face,
awkward but wholly ordinary,
this voice, which stuns him when he hears
to muteness, pure though momentary:

out of these fictions Finkel spins
a sharp-nosed, grinning, too-loud world
he shudders at, to think it turns,
minute by minute, slowly bald.

Four

SLEEPING BEAUTY

What is inescapable in this story   is the fact
that the thirteenth fairy   said what she said
'without greeting anyone   or even glancing
at the company'   the story goes further   it says
'she called out in a loud voice'   all that
about the twelfth fairy softening the curse
can be tossed aside   as a feeble attempt
to soothe the children   the twelve other fairies
for that matter   can be tossed aside   even the king
and the court   and the kingdom   can be tossed aside

What remains   is the old lady   no
even that can be tossed aside   what remains
is the woman   looking neither left nor right
what remains   is the loud voice saying
even if there is nobody to hear   'the Princess
shall prick herself with a distaff in her fifteenth year
and shall fall down dead'   there need in fact
not even be a princess

RAPUNZEL

Rapunzel means rampion   wild pretty edible at the root
it was rampion her mother craved   carrying her
and it was rampion she got   sending poor Father
into the terrible garden   but like any flower
Rapunzel was easily plucked   so for all her pains
mother had nothing in the end

The business of hair
is another story   and like most stories probably untrue
who knows what the witch was singing over her Rapunzel
that sounded to peasants   *let down your hair*
it was in any case   an unfortunate transformation
leaving behind   for generations of children
the image of an old lady shinnying up a tower

The athletic prince on the other hand   got the best
of the bargain   it is told that he wandered
for some years living on roots and berries   in this way
he came upon Rapunzel   who threw herself on him weeping
two of her tears fell upon his eyes   and thenceforward
he could see as well as ever   suddenly the story rings true

RUMPELSTILTSKIN

It is not possible to spin gold out of straw
you know that   I know that   but it was not so
in the old days   then people were slave
to a strange benevolent darkness   they thought
overnight   peasant girls could be turned into princesses
the King thought so   the miller thought so
even the miller's daughter thought so
she thought it was merely impossible for *her*   only
Rumpelstiltskin knew better   he knew however
that every morning   when the sun struck through the window
just so   the straw became gold as any gold
it is always given to men with ridiculous names
to keep worthless secrets like that   in a land of fools

It was this secret the new queen finally discovered
and not his name   which he did not utter simply
because it embarrassed him   once the truth was out
however   and it was clear that anybody could turn the trick
the Queen began to mock him with his name   Rumpelstiltskin
Rumpelstiltskin   she giggled   Rumpelstiltskin

LETTER TO MY DAUGHTER AT THE END OF HER SECOND YEAR

Now it is only hours before you wake
to your third year and to the gifts that lie
piled on the coffee-table, yet I keep
the only gift that it is mine to make.

But how can I offer, among the paper hats,
among the balloons and coloring books and dolls
gleaming with golden hair and the sweet primaries,
this shabby vision of myself seeking,
among these gestures and images, myself?
My gift is wrought, not in the fire of love,
but in the consuming egotism of night
that blots out daughter, lover, wife and friend,
a time to take, my darling, not to give.

So smear this book with the sweetness of your fingers,
and mock with your eyes the brightness of this doll;
come learn our urgent language and put on
mask after mask to match our smiling faces,
seeking what gestures and images may serve
to charm the tall world down from which we smile.

Standing there in the shadow of our gifts,
may you forgive the love that lugged them home,
then turn and take the gift I could not give—
the language of childhood looking for itself
under a mountain of masks and dolls—the poem.

BONES

We let the forsythia go one more day,
watching the shrivelled yellow duncecaps fall
in a half-circle of broken sunlight on the floor.
Like last week's leftovers; though no one will eat them,
for the crime of waste we take another whiff
before, at arm's length, we relinquish
our tenuous hold into the garbage can.

A week ago I tore two dozen switches
out of the great clump by the driveway,
careful not to disturb, like drops of water,
the dark buds perilous along their length.
We forced them. Some ring that phrase has. We tore
them where they stood and stood them naked
in a bowl, and watched them in synthetic spring
dress themselves and then undress again.
And then one more day we let them stand.

Though what a day mattered to them or us
I couldn't answer, snapping their slender backs
one by one to fit them in the garbage.
Was it the need to let the bare bones read their message
there against the pale wall like a Chinese
character for death-with-feet-in-water?
Outside much more where that came from
nods darkly still in the late winter wind.

The truth is, a man has to go out of his way
to choose three apples, a cup, and a butter-knife
for company at the bottom of love's ladder.
It would have been so much more soothing to think,
as long as one began with illusion in any case,
that he might as well live out his novitiate
watching some wench offer between two fingers
'the strawberry of her breast.'

Or how moral one felt
lifting again that limp form down from the tree,
whose Death was so much less dead than these
impersonal groceries, motionless on the table.
These apples will neither save nor curse;
their only virtues are, that they can be bought,
are edible till they rot, and will inform you,
if you choose to attend, that the world you move in
is round, palatable, composed, and incorrigibly itself.

When I first saw him, he was hanging by one leg
and thrashing against the window, his black
invincible thorax arched as if in death.
Of course, I couldn't hope to see his wings.

However, after a little time they stopped; swung
gently by the wind, he drew himself together
and opened his mouth. It was as if his head
had parted in the middle; he bit at the thread

that held him (or was it his leg?). Now, stretching
her downy delicate arms, she came downstairs;
she paused at the door to rearrange her hair.
He resumed thrashing. Lady that she was,

she turned her back, pretending not to see.
All this happened many times while I watched.
The thread held (or his leg), and as many times
as he ceased, she visited with him in his agony.

She went so far as to touch him once or twice,
lightly on the forehead. At which he thrashed.
Then suddenly, without reason, he left;
dropped like a stone from sight. Whether he flew

or fell I couldn't see. After a moment,
once more she crept downstairs to examine the spot,
made with her arms a few perfunctory gestures,
and then returned, tidying up the house.

SONIC BOOM

Nothing has happened, nothing has been broken,
everything is still in place, including yourself;
even now the juice of alarm begins to settle:
the bomber drags away her diminishing roar.
Nothing has happened; this was practice,
you are free to return. If there is a day
to come when you will be called out
to answer for somebody else's doings, this is not it.

Yet what is this delicate balance, that it shall not
be shaken? On the bookcase the figurine teeters;
which of its two thousand years gives it the right
to withstand one blow of the wind? Somewhere over
the plains an angel gathered enough speed
to outrun even the sound of her own voice.
In consequence, for miles around the night
exploded with the violence of her escape.
Yet she has not escaped. Behind her
and her ghostly silence, wherever she goes,
she drags like a harrow her unsettling past.

THE HUSBAND

When the man arrives tomorrow, bearing a token:
"Come, I will show you. Leave everything here;
dead weight; none of it matters," will I go?

A wife, two kids, my manuscripts, my car?
When I am eighty, and have outlived my debtors,
once more he will come. Then I'll go with him.

There is a dog barking somewhere down the street,
steadily, in snatches of three and four,
muffled, irregular, but continual.
I think of going downstairs, tracking him down,
my fury mounting as his barks grow louder,
and when I have found him, what will I not do?
But already the barks trail off, two,
a silence, one, now nothing, nothing
to stir me out of my chair, into the darkness.

THE FATHER

When I am walking with the children, and a girl
still hard in the buttocks bends to them with a laugh,
my heart bangs where it hangs in my empty carcase.
But you knew that. It has already passed
the stage of neighbors' gossip and attained
the clarity of an historical fact.
A myth comes down your street: here on my right
toddles my twinkling daughter, who loves me, while
on my left marches my son, who does not.

It is all true, but it does not matter;
in twenty years my son and I will have reached
a silent understanding, whereas (poor fool,
already growing hollow) some pimply bastard
will have made off with my blessings and my daughter.

FUNERAL PROCESSION

(AFTER RENÉ CLAIR)

Motionless, the camera eye allows
them to pass: the carriage glides over
the cobbles with a few involuntary shudders;
now the mourners, a silk formality of hats;
each simulates, with varying success,
the singleminded gravity of a wheel.
Their legs cause them a little difficulty,
also their children. The camera begins to peruse,
from carriage to mourners, and from mourners to carriage;
approaching, receding; now the carriage arrives;
or the mourners retreat. What have we seen?

Before we are certain, something imperceptible happens:
the mourners are walking with a new determination;
in the carriage some pressure is at work, it surges
toward the edge of the screen. Look: they rise up
on their toes, as if rebounding; the cobbles become
a sea of rubber balls; they leap, they dance.
The carriage is performing a series of jetés.

The cameraman tightens an invisible spring:
the mourners twitch like electrocuted frogs,
in their legs the strain of delight is beginning to tell,
one or two seem intent on reaching the carriage;
a rumor has gone out that the coffin is loose.
But the mourners will have none of it, they are running.

They manage to keep up. This new assurance
repays them for the loss of their dignity;
with élan, if with grace no longer, they enter the spirit
of the chase: at last they have found their part.

The ground has blurred to air; the great black kite
buffets on the wind, rises; the mourners trail,
a fluttering departure of rags and crepe.

MARRIAGE

The arrangement is essentially comic,
silent, and familiar to the audience:
you walk, and then I, six feet behind.
We are carrying something between us,
not visible, but obvious enough.

We are careful, though not beyond reason;
we do this every day. The audience
knows what to expect: the hero comes,
intent on his labors, of which we have
no part. Whatever he is doing,
we are only here to make things difficult;
that is, to go on doing what we are doing,
being careful, but not beyond reason.

You pass; always the gentleman, he waits.
Between you and me the distance is endless;
the audience catches its breath. Now.
Flattened against the glass his handsome
empty face registers the first flicker of surprise.

I pass. He will continue his labors;
he will return, presently, bearing
for the heroine a cluster of wilted flowers.
We go on. The audience no longer notices
that we continue to bear between us
something invisible, difficult to manage,
fragile, and slightly besmeared.

Five

THE KING, THE BLINDMAN, AND THE ELEPHANT

The king, as the custom ran, had been chosen to die,
despatched, in the name of the god, at the end of his reign.
From long meditation on this, he had grown most wise,
governed his people fairly, and knew their love.
The blindmen were everywhere, jabbing and shouting;
one sniffed a tusk, another kicked at a leg,
a third thrust an arm to the shoulder up the arse.
Fearing the prodigy might lose patience at last,
the king took pity and approached the quietest, who sat
with his back against a foreleg, nasally humming,
apparently a prayer. And you, he murmured,
what do you think the elephant is, a tree?
The old fellow paused in mid-measure, lifted his face,
the red slits of his eyes seemed to mimic a smile:
Put off, O Lord, thy question a little time;
blindness I have achieved, I am not yet wise.

Now the hubbub swelled, the king was forced to shout:
Do you want the truth? He is taller than two men;
he has a tail in front with which he uproots trees;
were he to raise his head, he would impale
three of you on each tusk; were he to run,
he would trample the lot of you like withered grass!
With this the king leapt back, for the old man threw
both fragile arms in the air and quavered out:
O the Lord be praised, for he is the fountain of mercy!
O the Lord be worshipped, he is a wall of concealment!
For we sit at the foot of destruction and are not destroyed,
for we thrust our arm in its arse and are not beshat;
for he hath vouchsafed us blindness, were man to see
the terrible monster of truth, he would not dare
one single faltering step on the path of wisdom!
In all of this, the elephant twitched not an ear.

SCRAWL AT THE ENTRANCE OF THE LABYRINTH

The priestess of Minos, Ariadne of the idolatrous breasts,
with two potions, one bitter, one sweet, and certain
ingenious manipulations in which she is versed,
can conjure you to a climax lasting days,
to a luxury so strenuous it is pain.

Beware of that maid and her supernatural breasts,
for in those frenzied hours a man will plead
for wilder and wilder perturbations. All
deftly she will provide, no matter how strained.

Seeking that climax to which the climax he suffers
is merely forepleasure, merely an amorous play,
probing the heart of his longing, he will exhume
all reeking carrion he had thought to hide;
he will bare himself to the bone, to the marrow of the bone.

BELMONTE

1
Had he Joselito's frame, he would have desired
nothing better than to conduct the sacrifice
with the same calm and purity of motion.

Called to his task, not born, hampered by doubts,
and a fine sense of his imperfections, he sought
new arrangements, new laws, a modern art.

Knowing the ritual must be at all costs preserved,
or man suffer the loss of his link with death,
he bade the priest assume the place of the bull.

As the bull leaned to the sword, he would lean to the horns,
proffering the secrets of his groin and breast;
he became the torero of three olés and an *ay!*

2
And what was it for the mob at the pyramid's foot
that the pampered hero, calm in his vegetable potions,
delivered up his heart to the ragged blade?

What was he worth, aloft, disdainful, withdrawn?
Yet they left released, as if from actual chains,
from the guilt which men call pity, from fear of death,

in the exhausted bliss that follows the creative act;
in that Sunday torpor they filed to their apartments;
for these he was victim, and not the stone-faced priests.

after the violence and visions, true smoker, sinks
into a world of his own, of shadows sharp
as knives, of strangers, and no use writing home,
having lost the language.

I speak of Rimbaud,
that sharp professor's baby, that shibboleth.
And still the punks complain: Why can't you shout,
'Oh, palms! Oh, garbage cans! Oh,
how I love my baby!' And I sink in my chair, wondering,
What other language can I speak? Rimbaud
is a word I know. I speak him. Is he less than a palm?

Among the racket and flies he walks, oh, palms!
oh, lovely kootch dancer in the drinking-tent!
Does he see nothing? Have his eyes been clouded by time?
Is he suddenly no longer the stranger? In the dark
pocket of his sex he watches the girl, offering,
thrusting, opening, closing. And does not speak.

1
Turned bronze in our fall, held on with rivets, it guards
the museum of desire against thieves, lovers, and the young.
Green, it was hardly more than a lady's whim;
the stripper's pastie clings with firmer intentions.

2
To lie is human, to say: I do not care;
to say, swollen with riches: I have nothing to give.
To cover like Venus is another thing altogether.
If she cared, she'd have worn her towel, or set her hounds
yapping at your throat. Canova's Venus at the Pitti
manages at least to hang a drape in the doorway.
(Her arms crush out the embers in her breast.)

3
The last veil of Salome, hesitant
long after she has proven her willingness:
from time to time see where her belly gleams,
the white moon glides behind her cloudy myth.

Underneath the breasts still beckon, the hips sway;
she has not the slightest intention of losing her power
merely because she has become more difficult of access.
Neither Rapunzel with her flowing hair,
nor Briar Rose of the downcast eye would dream
of such remoteness, the scent of her maidenhood
would not trouble the breeze somewhere in the country of men.

4
At the corrida she kept her eyes on the man.
It was as if, she said, her gaze was all
that hung like gauze between his heart and the horns.

She thinks, therefore he exists; true wife, sustainer,
cannot turn from the infant's cry, nor defy premonition.

She winds his boy-thin shoulders in a cape of thought
or settles on his sleep the blanket of her attention.

5
That the mind's laid open at all by the poem's edge,
that the temple's veil is rent by the cloudy sigh:
these miracles are the common sense of sense,
the word made flesh. For the mind can speak of trash,
and from that speech, from the mind's unwinding thread
weave silver trash: her veil is the mind's desire
made visible; it is to the mind the body owes her flesh.

Dying of his secret, he crept to the water's edge
on hands and knees. All night he dreamed, giddy
among the rushes, an ass swayed in the wind
twitching his ears. All night he heard the whisper
of lovers' thighs, and the grey rasp of the dead.
At the first glimmer of morning he thrust out his neck;
the cries pumped out of his blackness like rusted laughter.

Later, having thought better of it, sitting
in the great hall full of suppliants, he heard
someone whistle out in the yard the ass's lament.
The stream was clearer now, it purled out
into the sun, it leapt, it ran down the windows;
the curtains gleamed like cloth of gold. Soon
Midas himself was humming it. It was really quite catchy.

After a while it became the thing-in-itself:
in the granaries, the precious inedible wheat;
his sons grown brassy and arrogant; his daughters
unapproachable, without orifice, pure.
His wife was a reamed-out mine, exhausted earth:
all gold lay on the ground, spread out before him
in a broad glowing crust, like a valley of embers.

He kept on playing the market of possibilities
down to the last stock, himself; game
to the end, he ate gold, shat gold, picked from his nose.
Then slowly, one at last with the world, his treasure,
silent, grand, he sank in the glowing mass.

Leibniz was right, of course, and Voltaire wrong.
You cut off half an ass and it is still
the best of possible worlds. Because it happens;
because it is there, and we climb it. We die at the top,
on the slopes, frost-bitten, broken, chewing our shoes
for sustenance. (Against the sky the ridges
are sunlit and sharp as distinctions should be.) Because
we die. We teeter on the brink; we learn at last
how it never could have happened otherwise.

Yadwigha, girl of his youth, a little monkey-faced,
perhaps, but virginal; she stretches her arms along
the edge of the couch. Around her the jungle springs
fully armed with dangers. She holds them in the sway
of her dream, they stare; or freeze in conventional attitudes,
thinking of nothing. Out of the brush a green
flutist emerges, piping a tune as moist
and sinuous as a snake.

Perhaps he has gone
astray (can he dream her dream?), but it is hard
to tell if the flutist approaches, lover, or stays.
Or is it for the sweet old clerk he pipes? She waits,
lurking like music there in the underbrush.

He left me exposed on a hill of woman, my mother.
I paid him back at every crossroads, quitting
school, taking pot, writing poems
he couldn't fathom; after a while it palled.
The past is dead now, neither of us could care less.

But mamma, that's something else; no peace with *her*.
You can't turn your back, she is everywhere, under
your feet, like the ground. The old man's prod withdrawn,
she turns slowly inanimate; every year
she gets harder and harder to push away. It isn't
enough, any more, that she rarely calls. She is there;
and there's no getting around it, I am a bastard.

This country of visions, landscape of memory, where
it is possible to run down the stag, or stand, watching
the lovely princess imperceptibly breathe.
Down in the kitchen the cook and the scullery boy
have left off at last their immemorial squabble.

But sooner or later the stag is struck, or runs on;
the princess wakes and smiles and begins again
to speak and grow old. Downstairs the cook and the boy
make up, get married. Their squabble is endless.

Here
the rainbow and the rain are one. I catch
one drop in the eye's crystal, as it falls;
it hangs, prismatic, trivial, like a tear.

TALE

IN THE DARK WOODS, ON THE SODDEN GROUND, I FOUND MY WAY ONLY BY THE WHITENESS OF HIS COLLAR.

NOTE IN KAFKA'S DIARY

If the story is to prosper at all, the note must be both
a beginning and a center. So the scene is provided,
and the characters, the clothing of one, the weather, even
the outlines of the predicament, a glimmer of meaning.

As center, the scene and the predicament are one,
and probably the characters; they are all fused in a pellet.
Later they will open lazily upward, then outward
in all directions, like a Japanese water flower.

The scene is doubt, and the weather; at the center
the darkness is pervasive: both men are lost.
For what might a man in a collar do in such woods,
feeling the dampness come through his fine thin soles?

The prince rides after the stag-scut through bright green woods.
And supposing he finally reaches it, what can he want
from that unnatural laundry, an answer? God forbid.
He is only trailing the collar for someplace to go.

Back from the desert ordeal, gaunt, illumined,
even beautiful (why not?), his tale
is immediately recognizable to all.
Some will listen; some will not, yet follow;
and some will mutter and slay him, knowing well
what a reproach it is that he should see
what they have barely guessed. Though he tell all,
give all, even his life, he has not come back.
The myth comes back; he is still beyond the pale.

As if there were another place to go.
What did they mean? Or what did one
mean, and another take up, glad to know
he was not alone in how he saw that business?

Endlessly arriving and arriving;
and once there, well, one was there,
and nothing to do that time of night but sleep,
the gift shops closed, and bars and public buildings.

Or was it something shunned, and more like leaving?
And who left—it, or you? Somehow the difference
wore off along the way, and then you *were*
it, or it you.

Never so truly is man
no more than what he does. Without meditation,
dark in the mind as a mole, trembling; then
something muffled approaches, approaches. You wait,
though the world plunges about you as if in pain.

COMING: 2

Nothing can come up to it for making
one sure of his own existence. One is never
quite sure he has had a vision, felt an emotion,
written a poem, much less a perfect one.
But he can never doubt when he has come.

It never leaves you guessing. When you are born,
you are too young to know it. When you die,
Now I am dead, you say; but do you care?
And to neither can you return any better prepared.

But this is always open to perfection;
one can try and try till it is right:
the death, not only imminent, but chosen,
each day desired, each night enjoyed anew;
the birth, not only felt, but comprehended;
the poem, not only beautiful, but true.

LETTING GO

TO BE ON THE WIRE IS LIFE; THE REST IS WAITING.
KARL WALLENDA

One lets go of the platform, not the wire;
the walk is life. The times between are only
a kind of waking sleep, a death-in-life.

True, death is always there, night lady, lover
(grace of the bull-maid winding past the horn;
the numb ascent of the addict, out of life;
the dying backward of the poet into childhood,
walking the line half-drunk and mesmerized).

From the other platform, now, she comes, she glitters,
though under the lights no one can see her but you.
Both of you may as well fall now, as later:
back on the ground you will flush, as in shame, and bow.

TOPIARY

1 THE GARDENERS

Moist old earth, fat mother, flesh, we kneel
with our faces close to your cool black tit and prod
like schoolboys in a whorehouse, each alone,
sweating and frightened in his separate bed.

2 THE HEDGE-TRIMMER IN WINTER

You have worked free of yourselves, like stuffing from dolls;
or the hair of the dead, which goes on growing for days.
O my frowsy darlings! my brave free souls! the snow
hangs on your backs like clothes on careless boys.

How many times I soothed with my dreaming shears
that itch of wildness, that rage; and how you stood
respectfully in rows for the master's walk,
shining with dew so you might make him glad.

In the winter I shape in ice for the grand hotel.
One day each fall I wrap and tie with string
my tools and clothes, and go. A man must eat.
You knew full well I should return in spring.

Yet what has this tidy foresight gotten me?
Late every spring in my tiny room I kneel
and play with knots in the failing evening light
to loose the self-same pack I tied in fall:

my ancient clothes, my knives, my shears, my stone;
while outside on the lawn you toss together
(as if I had not been, as if, who knows?)—
unruly, ignorant, delicate as ever.

3 THE MANURE-SPREADER

Something made me slow down, weariness? boredom?
But only now, when the reeking barrow rolls
to a halt, can I see I've been laying it on too thick.
Then I pick up the handles again, and push like hell.

4 THE HEDGE-TRIMMER

Like the delicate labor by which a drunk ascends stairs,
the fragility of old men's hearts, the tug
of the questing broom in the house-maid's hands, or the dark
concentration of a boy peeing on a bug;

perfection, like justice, accomplishes nothing. Nor can
the slovenly earth abide for long the feel
of those smoothing, pinching, plucking hands, but will
wriggle her fat shoulders and fart like a seal.

DONALD FINKEL

Donald Finkel was born in New York City. He has a bachelor's degree in Philosophy and a master's degree in English Literature from Columbia University. At present teaching at Washington University in St. Louis, Missouri, Mr. Finkel also acts as poetry editor of the literary review, *MSS*. His first collection of poems, *The Clothing's New Emperor,* was published in 1959 in Scribner's series *Poets of Today VI*. He has published widely in literary magazines and is represented in several anthologies. In 1954 Mr. Finkel won first prize in a national poetry contest sponsored by the Philadelphia Art Alliance. The title poem of the present collection recently won the annual Helen Bullis prize, awarded through *Poetry Northwest* in which it was first published.